A. E. Gore.

THE SINLESS CHILD,

AND

OTHER POEMS,

BY

ELIZABETH OAKES SMITH.

EDITED BY

JOHN KEESE.

WILEY & PUTNAM, NEW YORK.
W. D. TICKNOR, BOSTON.

M DCCC XLIII.

HARVARD COLLEGE LIBRARY
SHELDON FUND
JULY 10, 1940

Entered according to Act of Congress, in the year eighteen hundred and forty three, by JOHN KEESE, in the Clerk's office of the District Court of the Southern District of New York.

D. Murphy, Printer, 384 Pearl Street.

THE SINLESS CHILD.

"I say unto you, that in heaven their angels do always behold the face of my Father, which is in heaven."—*Matthew*, xviii. 10.

TO THE READER.

Both the English reviews and our own periodicals, have made themselves so merry over the existing literary fashion of one friend editing the works of another, who still lives to write; that there can be no impertinence in the collector of these poems, "defining his position," while giving them to the public.

The three volumes, of a similar description, edited by him, were so cordially noticed by the press, that no stimulus was wanting in the farther indulgence of his taste in collecting American Poetry, the more especially, as the demi-professional character of Publisher, in which he was best known perhaps, seemed to oppose no bar to the courteous reception of his editorial labours among the literary fraternity.

And why, indeed, it may be observed in passing, should not a bookseller aim at being something more than the mechanical salesman of printed paper! Are *his* pursuits, of all others, the most hostile to literary culture? Is he presumed to exercise neither judgment nor taste in furthering the ends of trade; presumed to buy and sell only according to the existing demands of the literary market; while even the enterprise of the haberdasher is denied him, in anticipating the call for an article and introducing it to "the season."

Surely, in this country, at least, no pursuit is thus conducted; for while on the one side, the producer is constantly obliged to act as his own factor; on the other, whether it be the staple of cotton, or the fabrication of pin-heads, every intelligent dealer makes himself, more or less familiar with the processes of nature or of art, in the production of the article. In fact, whether the "operation," be in wheat or tobacco, in books or burlaps, it is this exercise of his own intelligence, which alone gives soul to enterprise, and distinguishes the energy of the operator from that of a mill-horse or steam-engine.

Now, after this formal, but he trusts, not presuming preamble, the writer is somewhat discomfitted at being compelled to acknowledge, that with regard to the publication of the present volume, he cannot claim the exercise of one particle of that literary discernment which he has been trying to persuade the reader is the gift of every successful publisher. The author of these admirable poems has, indeed, been long known to him as one of the most successful contributors to the popular magazines of the day. A woman whose varied powers have been proved in almost every department of periodical writing; a graceful, thinking, and vigorous essayist; a vivid narrator, whose humour, sentiment, and singularly felicitous descriptive powers, betrayed even in her most hurried effusions, a mastery of the whole gamut of thought, feeling, and expression. But as a poet, the author of the "Sinless Child," was scarcely known to him at the time he embodied, with others, the verses which appeared in one of his previous volumes;* and it was through his professional avocations only, that he was introduced to the rare work of genius which gives its title to the present volume.

The "Sinless Child," was first published in the Southern Literary Messenger, some eighteen

* The Poets of America, edited by John Keese, vol. 2.

months since. The manner in which it was received by the public is familiar to those who keep an eye upon the new developements of literary power, which are constantly appearing in our brief-lived, but thriving growth of national periodicals. The writer of this, cannot claim to have been among the first to welcome the advent of a fresh and original poem, whose inspiration seems drawn from the purest well-springs of thought and fancy; nay, as already hinted, he admits that it was only the frequent demand for the work at his publishing office, under the presumption that it had already assumed the form of a book, which induced him, in the first instance, to procure a copy, and make a personal examination of its beauties. He *does* claim, however, that in the many months which have passed away since that first perusal, no effort has been spared, upon his part, to have it brought before the public in a fitting shape. The hesitation and diffidence of the party chiefly interested in such a step, will be appreciated and understood by those who, living by their daily literary toil, and often giving their name to the public, with some hasty effusion, designed to meet the immediate call upon their pen, still preserve a high intellectual standard within their own minds, and distrust their best productions when put forth as the consummate effort of their literary powers.

It is with honest and heartfelt gratification therefore, that the writer of these remarks has availed himself of the high privilege of superintending the present volume, nor does he fear, that the act of introducing it to the public, under *his own name*, requires farther explanation or apology, with those who love pure poetry and respect womanly feeling.

J. K.

THE editor ought, perhaps, to content himself with giving the foregoing account of his incidental connection with the work now before the reader. It may be thought, however, that his share in bringing it before the public, were incomplete, without subjoining a more particular notice of the author and her productions.

In several attempts he has made to prepare this, he has never been able to succeed to his own satisfaction; on the one hand, the earnestness with which he would claim for her a foremost rank among the writers of the country, might be attributed to the zeal of personal friendship—while, on the other, appreciating the rare merit of these poems, as he does, he could not, with proper respect for his own opinions, speak in cold and measured words, of productions so rich in exquisite fancy and high moral beauty. He has, therefore, ventured to adopt here, the notices of two skilful writers, whose names, at least, will go far to authenticate his own judgment.

PREFACE.

The following lively sketch of the author of "The Sinless Child," (who is a native of Portland, Mass.) appeared sometime since in "The Family Companion;" when the varied literary powers of Mrs. Smith had, as yet, but partially developed themselves. It is interesting as a piece of literary biography, while highly characteristic of the racy writer from whose quaint, but fervid pen it originates. Mr. Neal, never too ready to praise, was one of the first, it is said, to hail the early promise of his gifted townswoman.

ELIZABETH OAKES SMITH,

BY JOHN NEAL.

Mrs. Seba, or properly speaking, Mrs. Elizabeth, is the wife of Mr. Seba Smith. Of the husband, as the only true and genuine, or as the Yankees have it, gin-or-wine, Jack Downing, and the unquestionable originator of that character, most of our people know something already. But, although multitudes may have heard of Mr. Seba Smith—if not by his own name, at least by that of Major Downing—it is the few, only—the very few—that have heard of Mr. Seba Smith's wife. And yet, no woman of our day, better deserves a more delicate and becoming notoriety.

Modest, pretty, loving and gentle, given to poetry—sincere and beautiful poetry—and writing very agreeable prose, too, at a pinch—witness her little roguish stories about Uncle Zeke, and others—always picturing what she sees with uncommon sprightliness and truth, one would'nt much wonder, perhaps, to find the character of Major Downing himself, the joint product of husband and wife. We have heard such things whispered heretofore, and are not quite sure that we havn't vouched for their truth, on being taxed ourself with the authorship of many a Yankee we never heard of. But, however that may be, it is quite impossible that such a woman as the wife, should associate long with such a man as the husband, both writing for their livelihood—and both in prose and poetry—without intermingling thoughts and hopes, and fancies, without helping and profiting one another; nor without influencing and tempering each the style of the other.

The husband of the pleasant tempered, industrious and highly gifted woman we are now to deal with, was a graduate of Bowdoin College, some twenty years ago. Being a sort of a Booth Bay proprietor, he couldn't afford to stay at home and take root on the sea shore; but started South—worked his passage, for aught we know, as most Yankees do, when they travel—rested for a time at Baltimore—found seeking a fortune, a poor business to follow for life—returned to New England, as all Yankees do, before they die, or afterwards—set himself down in Portland, somewhere down east— became the editor of the Argus, a clever political paper, (though always on the wrong side,) and after a while married Miss Elizabeth Prince —then about fifteen or sixteen—then, as if that were not enough, set up a daily paper, called the Portland Courier, which grew and flourished, as all newspapers do, till it is high time they were paid for—and then went to the dogs— as all newspapers do at last. In the Courier, first appeared the Jack Downing letters, which were afterwards collected, and republished by Lilly, Wait & Co.—with great advantage to the public—and none at all to the author—the publishers having failed in the midst of their most promising enterprises, and poor Smith getting hardly a bone to pick, where he ought to have realized hundreds, not to say thousands. It were absurd, now, to gainsay the truth and originality—and the homely strength of these delineations. The numberless imitators, and followers afar off—to say nothing of two or three, who, profiting by his over-sights and mistakes, outstripped their master, and wrote even better, and truer, and much droller Yankee than Smith himself did, before he knocked off the first time—have settled that question. That they were hugely overrated, nobody qualified to judge, would ever think of denying. But, that they were new and happy, significant, and well managed, and truthful enough to give the author a high character in the world of invention, it were alike false and foolish to say now, whatever the jaded public and the conscientious newspaper people, who have been certifying counterfeits for a half a dozen years, may think proper to believe. And the man who was capable of making a series of local papers, relating for a long while to the nobodies of a state legislature, attractive to the great reading world of America—a man who had sufficient dramatic power to individualize and embody the Yankee character, and give it not only a 'local habitation and a name,' but to persuade people afar off, as Smith has done, that the Major was a real personage, a bit of honest New England flesh and blood—we have heard, on respectable authority, of the Major's health being inquired after by a gentlemanly planter, who had met him at Washington, as he himself declared on hearing it intimated by the party he inquired of, that he had always looked upon the worthy

Major, as a sort of ideal personage—a man equal to all this, richly deserves to rank with De Foe, and Bunyan. There must be not only truth but originality and straight forward lusty strength in such portraitures.—Well, and so after a time, the husband—Seba Smith—or Major Jack Downing—for they are not only inseparable now, but identical—Smith answering to the name of Major Downing in public, and paying the Major's bills at sight—poor fellow! took it into his head to bait a trap with his own fingers—in other words, to dabble with Eastern lands.—The result was just what such a man, if he had a tithe of the shrewdness people credit him for as Major Jack, ought to have foreseen. He was ruined—lock, stock and barrel—horse, foot and dragoons—sinker and line; gave up his paper—or sold out, which—in a losing concern, where neutrality is sure to be trampled under foot, like a squeezed orange after the juice has been wrung out of it—amounts pretty much to the same thing. Thence to New York went he, bag and baggage—three children and a wife, the most delightful baggage on earth, under tolerable circumstances. There, husband and wife, having entered into copartnership for another term—though the first was forever—are trying to support themselves by their pen; he writing Powhattan—a metrical romance of singular beauty and simplicity, and as true as truth itself; and she Uncle Zeke, and other prose trifles, with some exquisite pages of womanly poetry, for the Ladies' Companion, and the Southern Literary Messenger.

And now, one word of Mrs. Smith herself. She is still young, not over thirty or thirty-two; and twenty years from to-day, if she lives, will be spoken of as the beautiful Mrs. Smith. It cannot be otherwise. Phrenologically speaking, her head is a picture, though the frontal developments are too large for a woman. With a fine complexion, clear, pleasant eyes, and very attractive manners, good health, one husband, and but three or four children, we believe—what on earth should prevent her being always beautiful, and always young?

If she but keeps her heart cool and fresh—her eyes 'unsullied by a tear,' that she would have been sorry for at sixteen—loving children, and the plays of children, as she does, and full of child-like sympathy—your truest milk of roses, after all—the dew of perpetual youth, the sunshine of the heart, must be upon her forever. If the aged wax young by sleeping with the newly born—why not by playing with them.

And now to the moral—that our countrywomen may be encouraged. When Miss

Elizabeth Prince—a mere child—married Mr. Seba Smith, who had been writing for the newspapers of the day, nobody knows how long, had she been asked if she ever hoped to equal her husband, or to contribute, in any way, to his reputation as a literary man, she would have laughed in your face. And long after that, years after she had begun to hazard little scraps of prose and poetry for her husband's newspaper, which he carefully corrected for her, if she had been questioned, she would have acknowledged, that so far from dreaming of what has since occurred, she would as soon think of enlisting for a drummer boy, or of digging clams at the halves, either at Cape Elizabeth, or Booth Bay, as of earning a dollar by the pen. Yet such has been her willingness and her energy; such her steadfast determination to do all that might become a woman, for the help of her husband, who has had every thing to struggle with since he removed to New York, and for the support of her little family, that she is now a regular, and we hope well paid, contributor to some of our cleverest and most popular Journals, and has won for herself a most desirable reputation. She was a child but the other day; with no sense of her own strength; and after she became a woman, her countenance you could not see for her veil, and her wings were hidden by her shawl. But the rains beat upon her husband, upon her little ones; and the winds blew, and the floods came, and lo! the veil and the shawl disappeared like the mists of summer; and the highest nature of woman broke forth like sunshine, and her wings were moulted, and her feet planted upon a rock, sure and steadfast. She no longer trembles when you look into her heart, or try to read her eyes; neither shawl or veil is wanted now. The woman is no longer ashamed or anxious to hide herself when called to by her Heavenly Father. She feels her own worth, and looks out, unswerving and self-dependent, upon the storms about her. What the girl and bride were unequal to, the wife and the mother delights to grapple with.

As a *pendant* of this vivacious sketch of Mr. Neal, the following brief, but beautiful, analysis of Mrs. Smith's genius and character, by H. T. Tuckerman, is subjoined. It formed one of a series of Literary Portraits, which appeared recently in Graham's magazine, and is characterised by the delicacy of perception and refinement of expression which distinguish Mr. Tuckerman's critical essays:

Mrs. Smith has long been a frequent and admired contributor to our literary periodicals, but the efforts upon which her reputation chiefly depends, are comparatively recent. "The Sinless Child," a poem in seven cantos, was published during the present year. It is designed to illustrate the spiritual agency of Life and Nature upon the soul of childhood. The abstract theory developed, partakes largely of Wordsworth's philosophy, but in its details, the story displays a fancifulness and glow wholly distinct from the bard of Rydal Mount. Eva is the heroine of this sweet tale:

> —" She turned the wheel,
>   Or toiled in humble guise,
> Her buoyant heart was all abroad
>   Beneath the pleasant skies.
> She sang all day from joy of heart,
>   For joy that in her dwelt,
> That unconfined the soul went forth—
>   Such blessedness she felt."

We refrain from entering more fully into the merits of this production, because it is about to be given to the public in a more permanent form. In point of elevated moral design and delicate beauty of imagery, we regard it as one of the most happy efforts of the American muse. Within a few weeks, a prose tale, intended to illustrate the times of Tecumseh, has appeared from her pen. This work has been widely commended for graphic descriptions of scenery and graceful simplicity of style.

Among the women of genius which this country has produced, there is none to whom we revert with more pride and kindly interest than the subject of this article. Rare endowments of mind, however brilliant, depend so much for their value upon the moral qualities with which they are united, that, abstractly considered, it is often difficult to decide whether they are a bane or a blessing. We may wonder at an intellectual phenomenon as we do at the extraordinary displays of nature, but it is only when a gifted mind is linked with noble sentiments and pure affections, that we can cordially hail it as a glorious boon. If this is true of men, how much more does it apply to women. What mental power or grace can atone for the absence of tenderness and truth in woman? What extent of attainment in a female mind can ever compensate for the lack of those sympathetic qualities in which consists the charm of the sex?

We make these inquiries, in order to fix the attention of our readers upon the truly feminine character of Mrs. Smith's genius. This we consider its peculiar distinction. There is a delicacy of conception, a simple grace of language, and an exaltation of sentiment about her writings, not only admirable in themselves, but beautifully appropriate to her character and mission as a woman. In a literary point of view, undoubtedly many of her productions bear the marks of haste. A higher finish and more careful revision would render the fruits of her pen more tasteful and permanent in their influence. But these defects are ascribable to circumstances rather than to want of perception or power. She has often written from the spur of necessity. He nature is one, which, in a more prosperous condition of things, would find its whole delight in expatiating amid the genialities of nature and society. She has resorted to the pen, rather as duty than a pleasure. We do not mean to say, that in any event she would not have written.— A mind of this order must, at times, " wreak itself upon expression." Mrs. Smith sympathizes too readily with the beautiful, not sometimes cordially to utter hymns in its praise. Human life presses with too deep a meaning upon her heart, not to leave results which crave utterance. To breathe such thoughts is as natural as for the glad bird to utter its song, or the unfettered stream to leap up to the sunshine. Still, friendship and nature, society and literature, would amply fill such a mind, were it indulged with the leisure and freedom from care, which fortune bestows. For the sake of poetry and the promotion of elevated views of life, we cannot mourn the destiny which made such a woman known to fame. We doubt not, that many of her sweet fancies and holy aspirations, winged by the periodical press over our broad land, have carried comfort to the desponding and bright glimpses to the perverted. We hope, that not a few of her sex have hailed these manifestations in language of what is highest in their own souls. For ourselves, we are happy to recognize in this lady, one who has given worthy utterance to sentiments of faith and duty, to the sense of the beautiful and the capacity of progress, which are the redeeming traits of human nature.

To the foregoing sketch of the *author* and analysis of her *genius*, the following discriminating notice of the *Poem* itself, seems a fitting accompaniment. It appeared originally in the Boston Notion, upon the first publication of the "The *Sinless Child.*"

The whole poem breathes the very air of purity, and is instinct with the life and soul of poetry. It is one of those productions which, without dazzling by brilliant points of expression or imagery, still wins upon the heart by the pure force of the sentiment embodied, and the naturalness and beauty of the language in which it is clothed. The object of the writer appears to be the exhibition of a pure and gentle being, whose mind and affections are so harmoniously developed and so beautifully blended, that every thing she sees takes the hue of her thoughts, and all outward nature moulds itself into accordance with her feelings; until the child, in her communings with nature, is supposed to see through the crust of creation, and to become cognizant of the spirit and moral meaning it contains.

It is a production, which, not only, in the current language of newspaper critics, does credit to the talents of its author, but it is an unconscious eulogy on the purity of her mind, for it is a work which demands more in its composition than mere imagination or intellect could furnish. The poem strongly suggests to the mind the beautiful lines of Wordsworth, in which he sets platonism to sweeter music than it has found since the time of its founder:

> " The soul that rises with us, our life's star,
>   Hath had elsewhere its setting,
>   And cometh from afar;
>   Not in entire forgetfulness,
>   And not in utter nakedness,
> But trailing clouds of glory do we come,
>   From God, who is our home."

THE
SINLESS CHILD.

THE SINLESS CHILD.

INSCRIPTION.

Sweet Eva! shall I send thee forth,
   To other hearts to speak?
With all thy timidness and love,
   Companionship to seek?
Send thee with all thy abstract ways,
   Thy more than earthly tone—
An exile, dearest, send thee forth,
   Thou, who art all mine own!

Thou art my spirit's cherished dream,
   Its pure ideal birth;
And thou hast nestled in my heart,
   With love that's not of earth.
Alas! for I have failed, methinks,
   Thy mystic life to trace;
Thy holiness of thought and soul,
   Thy wild enchanting grace.

With thee I've wandered, cherished one,
   At twilight's dreamy hour
To learn the language of the bird,
   The mystery of the flower;
And gloomy must that sorrow be,
   Which thou could'st not dispel,
As thoughtfully we loitered on
   By stream or sheltered dell.

Thou fond Ideal! vital made,
  The trusting, earnest, true;
Who fostered, sacred, undefiled
  My hearts pure, youthful dew;
Thou woman—soul, all tender, meek,
  Thou wilt not leave me now
To bear alone the weary thoughts
  That stamp an aching brow!

Yet go! I may not say farewell,
  For thou wilt not forsake,
Thou'lt linger, Eva, wilt thou not,
  All hallowed thoughts to wake?
Then go; and speak to kindred hearts
  In purity and truth;
And win the spirit back again,
  To Love, and Peace, and Youth.

PART I.

Eva, a simple cottage maiden, given to the world in the widowhood of one parent, and the angelic existence of the other, like a bud developed amid the sad sweet sunshine of autumn, when its sister-flowers are all sleeping, is found from her birth to be as meek and gentle as are those pale flowers that look imploringly upon us, blooming as they do apart from the season destined for their existence, and when those that should hold tender companionship with them have ceased to be. She is gifted with the power of interpreting the beautiful mysteries of our earth. The delicate pencilling found upon the petals of the flowers, she finds full of gentle wisdom, as well as beauty. The song of the bird is not merely the gushing forth of a nature too full of blessedness to be silent, but she finds it responsive to the great harp of the universe, whose every tone is wisdom and goodness. The humblest plant, the simplest insect, is each alive with truth. More than this, she beholds a divine agency in all things, carrying on the great purposes of love and wisdom by the aid of innumerable happy spirits, each delighting in the part assigned it. She sees the world, not merely with mortal eyes, but looks within to the pure internal life, of which the outward is but a type. Her mother, endowed with ordinary perceptions, fails to understand the high spiritual character of her daughter, but feels daily the truthfulness and purity of her life. The neighbors, too, feel that Eva is unlike her sex only in greater truth and elevation.

Whilom ago, in lowly life,
   Young Eva lived and smiled,
A fair-haired girl, of wondrous truth,
   And blameless from a child.
Gentle she was, and full of love,
   With voice exceeding sweet,
And eyes of dove-like tenderness,
   Where joy and sadness meet.

No Father's lip her brow had kissed,
   Or breathed for her a prayer;
The widowed breast on which she slept,
   Was full of doubt and care;
And oft was Eva's little cheek
   Heaved by her mother's sigh—
And oft the widow shrunk in fear
   From her sweet baby's eye,

For she would lift her pillowed head
   To look within her face,
With something of reproachfulness,
   As well as infant grace,—
A trembling lip, an earnest eye,
   Half smiling, half in tears,
As she would seek to comprehend
   The secret of her fears.

4

Her ways were gentle while a babe,
　With calm and tranquil eye,
That turned instinctively to seek
　The blueness of the sky.
A holy smile was on her lip
　Whenever sleep was there,
She slept, as sleeps the blossom, hushed
　Amid the silent air.

5

And ere she left with tottling steps
　The low-roofed cottage door,
The beetle and the cricket loved
　The young child on the floor,
And every insect dwelt secure
　Where little Eva played;
And piped for her its blithest song
　When she in greenwood strayed;

With wing of gauze and mailed coat
    They gathered round her feet,
Rejoiced, as are all gladsome things,
    A truthful soul to greet.
They taught her infant lips to sing
    With them a hymn of praise,
The song that in the woods is heard,
    Through the long summer days.

And everywhere the child was traced
    By snatches of wild song,
That marked her feet along the vale,
    Or hill-side, fleet and strong.
She knew the haunts of every bird—
    Where bloomed the sheltered flower,
So sheltered, that the searching frost
    Might scarcely find its bower.

1.

No loneliness did Eva know,
   Though playmates she had none;
Such sweet companionship was hers,
   She could not be alone;
For everything in earth or sky
   Caressed the little child,
The joyous bird upon the wing,
   The blossom in the wild:

2.

Much dwelt she on the green hill-side,
   And under forest tree;
Beside the running, babbling brook,
   Where lithe trout sported free—
She saw them dart, like stringed gems,
   Where the tangled roots were deep,
And learned that peace and love alone
   A joyous heart may keep.

The opening bud, that lightly swung
   Upon the dewy air,
Moved in its very sportiveness
   Beneath angelic care;
For pearly fingers gently oped
   Each curved and painted leaf,
And where the canker-worm had been
   Looked on with angel-grief.

She loved all simple flowers that sprung
   In grove or sun-lit dell,
And of each streak and varied hue,
   A meaning deep would tell;
For her a language was impressed
   On every leaf that grew,
And lines revealing brighter worlds
   That seraph fingers drew.

Each tiny leaf became a scroll
    Inscribed with holy truth,
A lesson that around the heart
    Should keep the dew of youth;
Bright missals from angelic throngs
    In every by-way left,
How were the earth of glory shorn,
    Were it of flowers bereft!

They tremble on the Alpine height;
    The fissured rock they press;
The desert wild, with heat and sand,
    Shares too, their blessedness,
And wheresoe'er the weary heart
    Turns in its dim despair,
The meek-eyed blossom upward looks
    Inviting it to prayer.

The widow's cot was rude and low,
  The sloping roof moss-grown;
And it would seem its quietude
  To every bird were known,
The winding vine its tendrils wove
  Round roof and oaken door,
And by the flickering light, the leaves
  Were painted on the floor.

No noxious reptile ever there
  A kindred being sought,
The good and beautiful alone
  Delighted in the spot.
The very winds were hushed to peace
  Within the quiet dell,
Or murmured through the rustling bough
  Like breathings of a shell.

16

The gay bird sang from sheltering tree,
  Gay blossoms clustered round,
And one small brook came dancing by,
  With a sweet tinkling sound,
It stained the far-off meadow green
  It leaped a rocky dell
Then resting by the cottage door,
  In liquid music fell.

17

Upon its breast white lilies slept,
  Of pure and wax-like hue,
And brilliant flowers upon the marge.
  Luxuriantly grew.
They were of rare and changeless birth,
  Nor needed toil nor care;
And many marvelled earth could yield
  Aught so exceeding fair.

18

Young Eva said, all noisome weeds
  Would pass from earth away,
When virtue in the human heart
  Held its predestined sway;
Exalted thoughts were always hers,
  Some deemed them strange and wild;
And hence in all the hamlets round,
  Her name of SINLESS CHILD.

19

Her mother said that Eva's lips
  Had never falsehood known;
No angry word had ever marred
  The music of their tone.
And truth spake out in every line
  Of her fair tranquil face,
Where Love and Peace, twin-dwelling pair,
  Had found a resting place.

She felt the freedom and the light
  The pure in heart may know—
Whose blessed privilege it is
  To walk with God below;
To understand the hidden things
  That others may not see,
To feel a life within the heart,
  And love and mystery.

PART II.

The widow, accustomed to forms, and content with the faith in which she has been reared, a faith which is habitual, rather than earnest and soul-requiring, leaves Eva to learn the wants and tendencies of the soul, by observing the harmony and beauty of the external world. Even from infancy she seems to have penetrated the spiritual through the material; to have beheld the heavenly, not through a glass darkly, but face to face, by means of that singleness and truth, that look within the veil. To the pure in heart alone is the promise, "They shall see God."

Untiring all the weary day
   The widow toiled with care,
And scarcely cleared her furrowed brow
   When came the hour of prayer;
The voices, that on every side,
   The prisoned soul call forth,
And bid it in its freedom walk,
   Rejoicing in the earth;

2

Fall idly on a deafened ear,
 A heart untaught to thrill
When music gusheth from the bird,
 Or from the crystal rill
That moves unheeding by the flower
 With its ministry of love,
That weeps not in the moonlight pale
 Nor silent stars above.

3

Alas! that round the human soul
 The cords of earth should bind,
That they should bind in darkness down
 The light—discerning mind—
That all its freshness, freedom, gone
 Its destiny forgot,
It should, in gloomy discontent,
 Bewail its bitter lot.

But Eva while she turned the wheel,
   Or toiled in homely guise,
With buoyant heart was all abroad,
   Beneath the pleasant skies;
And sang all day from joy of heart,
   From joy that in her dwelt,
While unconfined her soul went forth—
   Such blessedness she felt.

All lowly and familiar things
   In earth, or air, or sky,
A lesson brought to Eva's mind
   Of import deep and high;
She learned, from blossom in the wild,
   From bird upon the wing,
From silence and the midnight stars,
   Truth dwelt in every thing,

6

The careless winds that round her played
  Brought voices to her ear,
But Eva, pure in thought and soul,
  Dreamed never once of fear—
The whispered words of angel lips
  She heard in forest wild,
And many a holy spell they wrought,
  About the Sinless Child.

7

And much she loved the forest walk,
  Where round the shadows fell,
The solitude of mountain height,
  Or green and lovely dell;
The brook dispensing verdure round,
  And singing on its way,
Now coyly hid in fringe of green,
  Now sparkling in its play.

She early marked the butterfly,
   That gay, mysterious thing,
That, bursting from its prison-house
   Appeared on golden wing;
It had no voice to speak delight,
   Yet on the floweret's breast,
She saw it mute and motionless,
   In long, long rapture rest.

She said, that while the little shroud
   Beneath the casement hung,
A kindly spirit lingered near,
   As dimly there it swung;
That music sweet and low was heard
   To hail its perfect life,
And Eva felt that insect strange
   With wondrous truth was rife.

10

It crawled no more a sluggish thing
   Upon the lowly earth;
A brief, brief sleep, and then she saw
   A new and radiant birth,
And thus she learned without a doubt,
   That man from death would rise,
As did the butterfly on wings,
   To claim its native skies.

11.

The rainbow, bending o'er the storm,
   A beauteous language told;
For angels, twined with loving arms,
   She plainly might behold,
And in their glorious robes they bent
   To earth in wondrous love,
As they would lure the human soul
   To brighter things above.

The bird would leave the rocking branch
   Upon her hand to sing,
And upward turn its fearless eye
   And plume its glossy wing,
And Eva listened to its song,
   Till all the sense concealed
In that deep gushing forth of joy,
   Became to her revealed.

And when the bird would build its nest,
   A spirit from above
Directed all the pretty work,
   And filled its heart with love.
And she within the nest would peep
   Its colored eggs to see,
But never touch the dainty thing,
   For a thoughtful child was she.

Much Eva loved the twilight hour,
   When shadows gather round
And softer sings the little bird,
   And insect from the ground;
She felt that this within the heart
   Must be the hour of prayer,
For earth in its deep quietude
   Did own its Maker there.

The still moon in the saffron sky
   Hung out her silver thread,
And the bannered clouds in gorgeous folds
   A mantle round her spread.
The gentle stars came smiling out
   Upon the brilliant sky,
That looked a meet and glorious dome,
   For worship pure and high;

And Eva lingered, though the gloom
　　Had deepened into shade ;
And many thought that spirits came
　　To teach the Sinless Maid,
For oft her mother sought the child
　　Amid the forest glade,
And marvelled that in darksome glen,
　　So tranquilly she stayed.

For every jagged limb to her
　　A shadowy semblance hath,
Of spectres and distorted shapes,
　　That frown upon her path,
And mock her with their hideous eyes;
　　For when the soul is blind
To freedom, truth, and inward light,
　　Vague fears debase the mind :

But Eva, like a dreamer waked,
   Looked off upon the hill,
And murmured words of strange, sweet sound,
   As if there lingered still
Ethereal forms with whom she talked,
   Unseen by all beside;
And she, with earnest looks, besought
   The vision to abide.

'Oh Mother! Mother! do not speak,
   Or all will pass away,
The spirits leave the green-hill side,
   Where light the breezes play;
They sport no more by ringing brook,
   With daisy dreaming by;
Nor float upon the fleecy cloud
   That steals along the sky.

It grieves me much they never will
   A human look abide,
But veil themselves in silver mist
   By vale or mountain side.
I feel their presence round me still,
   Though none to sight appear;
I feel the motion of their wings,
   Their whispered language hear.

With silvery robe, and wings outspread,
   They passed me even now;
And gems and starry diadems
   Decked every radiant brow.
Intent were each on some kind work
   Of pity or of love,
Dispensing from their healing wings
   The blessings from above.

22.

With downy pinion they enfold
  The heart surcharged with wo,
And fan with balmy wing, the eye
  Whence floods of sorrow flow;
They bear, in golden censers up,
  That sacred gift, a tear;
By which is registered the griefs,
  Hearts may have suffered here.

23.

No inward pang, no yearning love
  Is lost to human hearts,
No anguish that the spirit feels,
  When bright winged hope departs;
Though in the mystery of life
  Discordant powers prevail;
That life itself be weariness,
  And sympathy may fail:

Yet all becomes a discipline,
    To lure us to the sky;
And angels bear the good it brings
    With fostering care on high;
Though others, weary at the watch,
    May sink to toil-spent sleep,
And we are left in solitude,
    And agony to weep:

Yet *they* with ministering zeal,
    The cup of healing bring,
And bear our love and gratitude
    Away, on heavenward wing;
And thus the inner life is wrought,
    The blending earth and heaven;
The love more earnest in its glow,
    Where much has been forgiven!

I would, dear Mother, thou could'st see
  Within this darksome veil,
That hides the spirit-land from thee,
  And makes our sunshine pale;
The toil of earth, its doubt and care,
  Would trifles seem to thee;
Repose would rest upon thy soul,
  And holy mystery.

Thou would'st behold protecting care
  To shield thee on thy way,
And ministers to guard thy feet,
  Lest erring, they should stray;
And order, sympathy and love,
  Would open to thine eye,
From simplest creature of the earth
  To seraph throned on high.

1.

E'en now I marked a radiant throng,
  On soft wing sailing by,
To soothe with hope the trembling heart,
  And cheer the dying eye;
They smiling passed the lesser sprites,
  Each on his work intent;
And love and holy joy I saw
  In every face were blent.

2.

The tender violets bent in smiles
  To the elves that sported nigh,
Tossing the drops of fragrant dew
  To scent the evening sky.
They kissed the rose in love and mirth,
  And its petals fairer grew,
A shower of pearly dust they brought,
  And over the lily threw.

A host flew round the mowing field,
  And they were showering down
The cooling spray on the early grass,
  Like diamonds o'er it thrown;
They gemm'd each leaf and quivering spear
  With pearls of liquid dew,
And bathed the stately forest tree,
  Till its robe was fresh and new.

I saw a meek-eyed creature curve
  The tulip's painted cup,
And bless with one soft kiss the urn,
  Then fold its petals up.
A finger rocked the young bird's nest
  As high on a branch it hung.
And the gleaming night-dew rattled down,
  Where the old dry leaf was flung.

Each and all, as its task is done,
　　Soars up with a joyous eye,
Bearing aloft some treasured gift—
　　An offering ON HIGH.
They bear the breath of the odorous flower,
　　The sound of the bright-sea shell;
And thus they add to the holy joys
　　Of the home where spirits dwell.

PART III.

The grace of the soul is sure to impart expressiveness and beauty to the face. It must beam through its external veil; and daily, as the material becomes subordidate to the spiritual, will its transparency increase. Eva was lovely, for the spirit of love folded its wings upon her breast. All nature administered to her beauty; and angelic teachings revealed whence came the power that winneth all hearts. The mother is aware of the spell resting upon her daughter, or rather, that which seemed a spell to her, but which, in truth, was nothing more than fidelity to the rights of the soul, obedience to the voice uttered in that holy of holies. Unable to comprehend the truthfulness of her character, she almost recoils from its gentle revealings. Alas! that to assimilate to the good and beautiful should debar us from human sympathy! Eva walked in an atmosphere of light, and images of surpassing sweetness were ever presented to her eye. The dark and distorted shapes that haunt the vision of the unenlightened and the erring, dared not approach her. She wept over the blindness of her mother, and tenderly revealed to her the great truths that pressed upon her own mind, and the freedom and the light in which the soul might be preserved. She blamed not the errors into which weak humanity is prone to be betrayed, but deplored that it should thus blind its own spiritual vision, and thus impress dark and ineffaceable characters upon the soul; and thus sink, where it should soar.

As years passed on, no wonder, each
    An inward grace revealed;
For where the soul is peace and love,
    It may not be concealed.
They stamp a beauty on the brow,
    A softness on the face,
And give to every wavy line
    A tenderness and grace.

2

Long golden hair in many curls
  Waved o'er young Eva's brow;
Imparting depth to her soft eye,
  And pressed her neck of snow:
Her cheek was pale with lofty thought,
  And calm her maiden air;
And all who heard her birdlike voice,
  Felt harmony was there.

3

And winning were her household ways,
  Her step was prompt and light,
To save her mother's weary tread,
  Till came the welcome night;
And though the toil might useless be,
  The housewife's busy skill,
Enough for Eva that it bore
  Inscribed a mother's will;

4

For humble things exalted grow
  By sentiment impressed—
The love that bathes the way-worn feet,
  Or leans upon the breast;
For love, whate'er its offering be,
  Lives in a hallowed air,
And holy hearts before its shrine,
  Alone may worship there.

5

Young Eva's cheek was lily pale,
  Her look was scarce of earth,
And doubtingly the mother spoke,
  Who gave to Eva birth.
" O Eva, leave thy thoughtful ways,
  And dance and sing, my child;
For thy pallid cheek is tinged with blue,
  Thy words are strange and wild.

6

Thy father died—a widow left,
  An orphan birth was thine,
I longed to see thy infant eyes
  Look upward into mine.
I hoped upon thy sweet young face,
  Thy father's look to see;
But Eva, Eva, sadly strange
  Are all thy ways to me.

7

While yet a child, thy look would hold
  Communion with the sky;
Too tranquil is thy maiden air;
  The glances of thine eye
Are such as make me turn away,
  E'en with a shuddering dread,
As if my very soul might be
  By thy pure spirit read."

Slow swelled a tear from Eva's lid,
   She kissed her mother's cheek,
She answered with an earnest look,
   And accents low and meek :—
"Dear mother, why should mortals seek
   Emotions to conceal?
As if to be revealed were worse
   Than inwardly to feel.

The human eye I may not fear,
   It is the light within,
That traces on the growing soul
   All thought, and every sin.
That mystic book, the human soul,
   Where every trace remains,
The record of all thoughts and deeds,
   The record of all stains.

10

Dear mother! in ourselves is hid
    The holy spirit-land,
Where Thought, the flaming cherub, stands
    With its relentless brand;
We feel the pang when that dread sword
    Inscribes the hidden sin,
And turneth every where to guard
    The paradise within."

11

"Nay, Eva, leave these solemn words,
    Fit for a churchman's tongue,
And let me see thee deck thy hair,
    A maiden blithe and young.
When others win admiring eyes,
    And looks that speak of love,
Why dost thou stand in thoughful guise?
    Why cold and silent move?

76   THE SINLESS CHILD.

12

Thy beauty sure should win for thee
   Full many a lover's sigh,
But on thy brow there is no pride,
   Nor in thy placid eye.
Dear Eva! learn to look and love,
   And claim a lover's prayer,
Thou art too cold for one so young,
   So gentle and so fair."

13

" Nay, mother! I must be alone,
   With no companion here,
None, none to joy when I am glad,
   With me to shed a tear;
For who would clasp a maiden's hand
   In grot or sheltering grove,
If one unearthly gift should bar
   All sympathy and love!

14

Such gift is mine, the gift of thought,
　Whence all will shrink away,
E'en thou from thy poor child dost turn,
　With doubting and dismay.
And who shall love, and who shall trust,
　Since she who gave me birth,
Knows not the child that prattled once
　Beside her lonely hearth?

15

I would I were, for thy dear sake,
　What thou would'st have me be;
Thou dost not comprehend the bliss
　That's given unto me;
That union of the thought and soul
　With all that's good and bright,
The blessedness of earth and sky,
　The growing truth and light.

That reading of all hidden things
   All mystery of life,
Its many hopes, its many fears,
   The sorrow and the strife.
A spirit to behold in all,
   To guide, admonish, cheer,
Forever in all time and place,
   To feel an angel near."

" Dear Eva! lean upon my breast,
   And let me press thy hand,
That I may hear thee talk awhile
   Of thy own spirit-land.
And yet I would the pleasant sun
   Were shining in the sky,
The blithe birds singing through the air,
   And busy life, were by.

18

For when in converse, like to this,
　　Thy low, sweet voice I hear,
Strange shudderings o'er my senses creep,
　　Like touch of spirits near,
And fearful grow familiar things,
　　In silence and the night,
The cricket piping in the hearth,
　　Half fills me with affright.

19

I hear the old trees creak and sway,
　　And shiver in the blast;
I hear the wailing of the wind,
　　As if the dead swept past.
Dear Eva! 'tis a world of gloom,
　　The grave is dark and drear,
We scarce begin to taste of life
　　Ere death is standing near."

Then Eva kissed her mother's cheek,
   And look'd with sadden'd smile,
Upon her terror-stricken face,
   And talked with her the while;
And O! her face was pale and sweet,
   Though deep, deep thought was there,
And sadly calm her low-toned voice
   For one so young and fair.

"Nay mother, everywhere is hid
   A beauty and delight,
The shadow lies upon the heart,
   The gloom upon the sight;
Send but the spirit on its way
   Communion high to hold,
And bursting from the earth and sky,
   A glory we behold!

And did we but our primal state
  Of purity retain,
We might, as in our Eden days,
  With angels walk again.
And memories strange of other times
  Would break upon the mind,
The linkings, that the present join,
  To what is left behind.

The little child at dawn of life
  A holy impress bears,
The signet-mark by heaven affixed
  Upon his forehead wears;
And nought that impress can efface,
  Save his own wilful sin,
Which first begins to draw the veil
  That shuts the spirit in.

And one by one its lights decay,
  Its visions tend to earth,
Till all those holy forms have fled
  That gathered round his birth;
Or dim and faintly may they come,
  Like memories of a dream,
Or come to blanch his cheek with fear,
  So shadow-like they seem.

And thus all doubtingly he lives
  Amid his gloomy fears,
And feels within his inmost soul,
  Earth is a vale of tears:
And scarce his darkened thoughts may trace
  The mystery within;
For faintly gleams the spirit forth
  When shadow'd o'er by sin.

26.

Unrobed, majestic, should the soul
  Before its God appear,
Undimmed the image He affixed,
  Unknowing doubt or fear;
And open converse should it hold,
  With meek and trusting brow;
Such as man was in Paradise
  He may be even now.

27.

But when the deathless soul is sunk
  To depths of guilt and wo,
It then a dark communion holds
  With spirits from below."
And Eva shuddered as she told
  How every heaven-born trace
Of goodness in the human soul
  Might wickedness efface.

Alas! unknowing what he doth,
  A judgment-seat man rears,
A stern tribunal throned within,
  Before which he appears;
And conscience, minister of wrath,
  Approves him or condemns,
He knoweth not the fearful risk,
  Who inward light contemns.

"O veil thy face, pure child of God,"
  With solemn tone she said,
"And judge not thou, but lowly weep,
  That virtue should be dead!
Weep thou with prayer and holy fear,
  That o'er thy brother's soul,
Effacing life, and light and love,
  Polluting waves should roll.

Weep for the fettered slave of sense,
　　For passion's minion weep!
For him who nurtureth the worm,
　　In death that may not sleep;
And tears of blood, if it may be,
　　For him, who plunged in guilt,
Perils his own and victim's soul,
　　When human blood is spilt.

For him no glory may abide
　　In earth or tranquil sky,
Fearful to him the human face,
　　The searching human eye.
A light beams on him everywhere;
　　Revealing in its ray,
An erring, terror-stricken soul,
　　Launched from its orb away.

Turn where he will, all day he meets
   That cold and leaden stare;
His victim pale, and bathed in blood,
   Is with him everywhere;
He sees that shape upon the cloud,
   It glares from out the brook,
The mist upon the mountain side,
   Assumes that fearful look.

He sees, in every simple flower,
   Those dying eyes gleam out;
And starts to hear that dying groan,
   Amid some merry shout.
The phantom comes to chill the warmth,
   Of every sunlight ray,
He feels it slowly glide along,
   Where forest shadows play.

And when the solemn night comes down,
 With silence dark and drear,
His curdling blood and rising hair
 Attest the victim near.
With hideous dreams and terrors wild,
 His brain from sleep is kept,
For on his pillow, side by side,
 That gory form hath slept."

"O Eva, Eva, say no more,
 For I am filled with fear;
Dim shadows move along the wall;
 Dost thou not see them here?—
Dost thou not mark the gleams of light,
 The shadowy forms move by?"
"Yes, mother, beautiful to see!
 And they are always nigh.

O, would the veil for thee were raised
   That hides the spirit-land,
For we are spirits draped in flesh,
   Communing with that band;
And it were weariness to me,
   Were only human eyes
To meet my own with tenderness,
   In earth or pleasant skies."

PART IV.

The widow, awe-struck at the revealments of her daughter, is desirous to learn more; for it is the nature of the soul to search into its own mysteries: however dim may be its spiritual perception, it still earnestly seeks to look into the deep and the hidden. The light is within itself, and it becomes more and more clear at every step of its progress, in search of the true and the beautiful. The widow, hardly discerning this light, which is to grow brighter and brighter to the perfect day, calls for the material lights that minister to the external eye; that thus she may be hid from those other lights that delight the vision of her child. Eva tells of that mystic book—the human soul—upon which, thoughts, shaped into deeds, whether externally, or only in its own secret chambers, inscribe a character that must be eternal. But it is not every character that is thus clearly defined as good or evil. Few, indeed, seize upon thought, and bring its properties palpably before them. Impressions are allowed to come and go with a sort of lethargic indifference, leaving no definite lines behind, but only a moral haziness. The widow recollects the story of old Richard, and Eva supplies portions unknown to her mother, and enlarges upon the power of conscience, that fearful judge placed by the Infinite within the soul, with the two-fold power of decision, and punishment.

" Then trim the lights, my strange, strange child,
   And let the faggots glow;
For more of these mysterious things
   I fear, yet long, to know.
I glory in thy lofty thought,
   Thy beauty and thy worth,
But, Eva, I should love thee more,
   Did'st thou seem more like earth."

A pang her words poor Eva gave,
  And tears were in her eye,
She kissed her mother's anxious brow,
  And answered with a sigh;—
"Alas! I may not hope on earth
  Companionship to find,
Alone must be the pure in heart,
  Alone the high in mind!

We toil for earth, its shadowy veil
  Envelops soul and thought,
And hides that discipline and life,
  Within our being wrought.
We chain the thought, we shroud the soul,
  And backward turn our glance,
When onward should its vision be,
  And upward its advance.

I may not scorn the spirit's rights,
   For I have seen it rise,
All written o'er with thought, thought, thought,
   As with a thousand eyes!
The records dark of other years,
   All uneffaced remain;
Unchecked desire forgotten long,
   With its eternal stain.

Recorded thoughts, recorded deeds,
   Its character attest,
No garment hides the startling truth,
   Nor screens the naked breast.
The thought, fore-shaping evil deeds,
   The spirit may not hide,
It stands amid that searching light,
   Which sin may not abide.

6.

And never may the spirit turn
 From that effulgent ray,
It lives for ever in the glare
 Of an eternal day;
Lives in that penetrating light,
 A kindred glow to raise,
Or every withering sin to trace
 Within its searching blaze.

7.

Few, few the shapely temple rear,
 For God's abiding place—
That mystic temple, where no sound
 Within the hallowed space
Reveals the skill of builder's hand;
 Yet with a silent care
That holy temple riseth up,
 And God is dwelling there. (*a*)

Then weep not when the infant lies.
   In its small grave to rest,
With scented flowers springing forth
   From out its quiet breast;
A pure, pure soul to earth was given,
   Yet may not thus remain;
Rejoice that it is rendered back,
   Without a single stain.

Bright cherubs bear the babe away
   With many a fond embrace,
And beauty, all unknown to earth,
   Upon its features trace.
They teach it knowledge from the fount,
   And holy truth and love;
The songs of praise the infant learns,
   As angels sing above."

The widow rose, and on the blaze
    The crackling faggots threw—
And then to her maternal breast
    Her gentle daughter drew.
"Dear Eva! when old Richard died,
    In madness fierce and wild,
Why did he in his phrenzy rave
    About a murdered child!

He died in beggary and rags,
    Friendless and grey, and old;
Yet he was once a thriving man,
    Light-hearted, too, I'm told.
Dark deeds were whispered years ago,
    But nothing came to light;
He seemed the victim of a spell,
    That nothing would go right.

12

His young wife died, and her last words
 Were breathed to him alone,
But 'twas a piteous sound to hear
 Her faint, heart-rending moan.
Some thought, in dreams he had divulged
 A secret hidden crime,
Which she concealed with breaking heart,
 Unto her dying time.

13

From that day forth he never smiled;
 Morose and silent grown,
He wandered unfrequented ways,
 A moody man and lone.
The schoolboy shuddered in the wood,
 When he old Richard passed,
And hurried on, while fearful looks
 He o'er his shoulder cast.

THE SINLESS CHILD. 97

14
And nought could lure him from his mood,
 Save his own trusting boy,
Who climbed the silent father's neck,
 With ministry of joy,
That gentle boy, unlike a child,
 Companions never sought,
Content to share his father's crust,
 His father's gloomy lot.

15
With weary foot and tattered robe,
 Beside him, day by day,
He roamed the forest and the hill,
 And o'er the rough highway;
And he would prattle all the time
 Of things to childhood sweet;
Of singing bird, or lovely flower,
 That sprang beneath their feet.

Sometimes he chid the moody man,
   With childhood's fond appeal :—
'Dear father, talk to me awhile,
   How very lone I feel!
My mother used to smile so sad,
   And talk and kiss my cheek,
And sing to me such pretty songs;
   So low and gently speak.

Then Richard took him in his arms
   With passionate embrace,
And with an aching tenderness
   He gazed upon his face;—
Tears rushed into his hollow eyes,
   He murmured soft and wild,
And kissed with more than woman's love
   The fond but frightened child.

He died, that worn and weary boy;
　And they that saw him die,
Said, on his father's rigid brow
　Was fixed his fading eye.
His little stiffening hand was laid
　Within poor Richard's grasp;—
And when he stooped for one last kiss,
　He took his dying gasp.

It crazed his brain,—poor Richard rose
　A maniac fierce and wild,
Who mouthed and muttered everywhere,
　About a murdered child."
" And well he might," young Eva said,
　" For conscience, day by day,
Commenced that retribution here,
　That filled him with dismay.

Unwedded, but a mother grown,
   Poor Lucy pressed her child,
With blushing cheek and dropping lid,
   And lip that never smiled.
Their wants were few; but Richard's hand
   Must buy them daily bread,
And fain would Lucy have been laid
   In silence with the dead.

For want, and scorn, and blighted fame
   Had done the work of years,
And oft she knelt in lowly prayer,
   In penitence and tears;
That undesired child of shame,
   Brought comfort to her heart,
A childlike smile to her pale lip,
   By its sweet baby art.

22

And yet, as years their passage told,
  Faint shadows slowly crept
Upon the blighted maiden's mind,
  And oft she knelt and wept
Unknowing why, her wavy form
  So thin and reed-like grew,
And so appealing her blue eyes,
  They tears from others drew.

23

Years passed away, and Lucy's child,
  A noble stripling grown,
A daring boy with chesnut hair,
  And eyes of changeful brown,
Had won the love of every heart,
  So gentle was his air,
All felt, whate'er might be his birth,
  A stainless heart was there.

The boy was missing, none could tell
    Where last he had been seen;—
They searched the river many a day,
    And every forest screen;
But never more his filial voice
    Poor Lucy's heart might cheer;
Lorn in her grief, and dull with wo,
    She never shed a tear.

And every day, whate'er the sky,
    With head upon her knees,
And hair neglected, streaming out
    Upon the passing breeze,
She sat beneath a slender tree
    That near the river grew,
And on the stream its pendant limbs
    Their penciled shadows threw.

26

The matron left her busy toil,
　And called her child from play,
And gifts for the lone mourner there
　She sent with him away.
The boy with nuts and fruit returned,
　Found in the forest deep,
A portion of his little store
　Would for poor Lucy keep.

27

That tree, with wonder all beheld,
　Its growth was strange and rare;
The wintry winds, that wailing passed,
　Scarce left its branches bare,
And round its roots a verdant spot
　Knew neither change nor blight,
And so poor Lucy's resting place
　Was alway green and bright.

Some said its bole more rapid grew
   From Lucy's bleeding heart,
For, sighs from out the heart, 'tis said,
   A drop of blood will start. (*b*)
It was an instinct deep and high
   Which led that Mother there,
And that tall tree aspiring grew,
   By more than dew or air.

The winds were hushed, the little bird
   Scarce gave a nestling sound,
The warm air slept along the hill,
   The blossoms drooped around;
The shrill-toned insect scarcely stirred
   The dry and crispéd leaf;
The laborer laid his sickle down
   Beside the bending sheaf.

A dark, portentous cloud is seen
   To mount the eastern sky,
The deep-toned thunder rolling on,
   Proclaims the tempest nigh!
And now it breaks with deafening crash,
   And lightnings livid glow;
The torrents leap from mountain crags
   And wildly dash below.

Behold the tree! its strength is bowed
   A shattered mass it lies;
What brings old Richard to the spot,
   With wild and blood-shot eyes?
Poor Lucy's form is lifeless there,
   And yet he turns away,
To where a heap of mouldering bones
   Beneath the strong roots lay.

Why takes he up, with shrivelled hands,
    The riven root and stone,
And spreads them with a trembling haste
    Upon each damp, grey bone.
It may not be, the whirlwind's rage
    Again hath left them bare,
Earth hides no more the horrid truth,
    A murdered child lies there!

Of wife, and child, and friends bereft,
    And all that inward light,
Which calmly guides the white-haired man,
    Who listens to the right;
Old Richard laid him down to die,
    Himself his only foe,
His baffled nature groaning out
    Its weight of inward wo."

PART V.

The storm is raging without the dwelling of the widow, but all is tranquil within. Eva hath gone forth in spiritual vision, and beheld the cruelty engendered by wealth and luxury—the cruelty of a selfish and unsympathizing heart. She relates what she has seen to her mother—The vision of the neglected children and their affluent stepmother. Sins of omission are often as terrible in their consequences, and as frightful in the retribution as crimes committed intentionally. Certain qualities of the heart are of such a nature, that, when in excess, they resolve themselves into appropriate forms. The symbol of evil becomes mentally identified with its substance, and the fearful shapes thus created haunt the vision like realities. The injurer is always fearful of the injured. No wrong is ever done with a sense of security; least of all, wrong to the innocent and unoffending. The belief of a Protecting Power watching over infancy, is almost universal; its agency being recognized even by those who have forgone the blessing in their own behalf. The little child is a mystery of gentleness and love, while it is preserved in its own atmosphere; and it is a fearful thing to turn its young heart to bitterness; to infuse sorrow and fear, where the elements should be only joy and faith. In maturer years, it is ever the state of the soul, the prevailing motive—the essential character that involves human peace or wretchedness. "The Kingdom of Heaven is within you," said the Great Teacher; and as we wander from the innocence of children, and allow selfishness or vice to increase upon the domain of the holy, distrust usurps the place of confidence and joy.

The loud winds rattled at the door—
   The shutters creaked and shook,
While Eva, by the cottage hearth,
   Sat with abstracted look.
With every gust, the big rain-drops
   Upon the casement beat,
How doubly, on a night like this,
   Are home and comfort sweet!

2

The maiden slowly raised her eyes,
   And pressed her pallid brow:—
"Dear mother! I have been far hence:
   My sight is absent now!
O mother! 'tis a fearful thing,
   A human heart to wrong,
To plant a sadness on the lip,
   Where smiles and peace belong.

3
In selfishness or callous pride,
   The sacred tear to start,
Or lightest finger dare to press
   Upon the burdened heart.
And doubly fearful, when a child
   Lifts its imploring eye,
And deprecates the cruel wrath
   With childhood's pleading cry.

The child is made for smiles and joy,
  Sweet emigrant from heaven,
The sinless brow and trusting heart,
  To lure us there, were given.
Then who shall dare its simple faith
  And loving heart to chill,
Or its frank, upward, beaming eye
  With sorrowing tears to fill!

I look within a gorgeous room,
  A lofty dame behold,
A lady with forbiding air,
  And forehead, high and cold;
I hear an infant's plaintive voice,
  For grief hath brought it fears,
None soothe it with a kind caress,
  None wipe away its tears.

6

His sister hears with pitying heart
  Her brothers wailing cry,
And on the stately step-dame turns
  Her earnest, tearful eye.
O lady, chilling is the air,
  And fearful is the night,
Dear brother fears to be alone,
  I'll bring him to the light.

7

On our dead mother hear him call;
  I hear him weeping say,
Sweet mother, kiss poor Eddy's cheek,
  And wipe his tears away.'
Red grows the lady's brow with rage,
  And yet she feels a strife
Of anger and of terror too,
  At thought of that dead wife.

Wild roars the wind, the lights burn blue,
   The watch-dog howls with fear,
Loud neighs the steed from out the stall:
   What form is gliding near?
No latch is raised, no step is heard,
   But a phantom fills the space,—
A sheeted spectre from the dead,
   With cold and leaden face.

What boots it that no other eye
   Beheld the shade appear!
The guilty lady's guilty soul
   Beheld it plain and clear,
It slowly glides within the room,
   And sadly looks around—
And stooping, kissed her daughter's cheek
   With lips that gave no sound.

Then softly on the step-dame's arm
    She laid a death-cold hand,
Yet it hath scorched within the flesh
    Like to a burning brand.
And gliding on with noiseless foot,
    O'er winding stair and hall,
She nears the chamber where is heard
    Her infant's trembling call.

She smoothed the pillow where he lay,
    She warmly tucked the bed,
She wiped his tears, and stroked the curls
    That clustered round his head.
The child, caressed, unknowing fear,
    Hath nestled him to rest;
The Mother folds her wings beside—
    The Mother from the Blest! (c)

Fast by the eternal throne of God
  Celestial beings stand,
Beings, who guide the little child
  With kind and loving hand:
And wo to him who dares to turn
  The infant foot aside,
Or shroud the light that ever should
  Within his soul abide."

PART VI.

It is the noon of summer, and the noonday of Eva's earthly existence. She hath held communion with all that is great and beautiful in nature, till it hath become a part of her being; till her spirit hath acquired strength and maturity, and been reared to a beautiful and harmonious temple, in which the true and the good delight to dwell. Then cometh the mystery of womanhood; its gentle going forth of the affections seeking for that holiest of companionship, a kindred spirit, responding to all its finer essences, and yet lifting it above itself. Eva had listened to this voice of her woman's nature; and sweet visions had visited her pillow. Unknown to the external vision, there was one ever present to the soul; and when he erred, she had felt a lowly sorrow that, while it still more perfected her own nature, went forth to swell likewise the amount of good in the great universe of God. At length Albert Linne, a gay youth, whose errors are those of an ardent and inexperienced nature, rather than of an assenting will, meets Eva sleeping under the canopy of the great woods, and he is at once awed by the purity that enshrouds her. He is lifted to the contemplation of the good—to a sense of the wants of his better nature. Eva awakes and recognizes the spirit that forever and ever is to be one with hers; that is to complete that mystic marriage, known in the Paradise of God; that marriage of soul with soul. Eva the pure minded, the lofty in thought, and great in soul, recoiled not from the errors of him who was to be made mete for the kingdom of Heaven, through her gentle agency, for the mission of the good and the lovely, is not to the good, but to the sinful. The mission of woman, is to the erring of man.

'Tis the summer prime, when the noiseless air
   In perfumed chalice lies,
And the bee goes by with a lazy hum
   Beneath the sleeping skies:
When the brook is low, and the ripples bright,
   As down the stream they go;
The pebbles are dry on the upper side,
   And dark and wet below.

2

The tree that stood where the soil's athirst,
　And the mulleins first appear,
Hath a dry and rusty colored bark,
　And its leaves are curled and sere;
But the dog-wood and the hazel bush,
　Have clustered round the brook—
Their roots have stricken deep beneath,
　And they have a verdant look.

3

To the juicy leaf the grasshopper clings,
　And he gnaws it like a file,
The naked stalks are withering by,
　Where he has been erewhile.
The cricket hops on the glistering rock,
　Or pipes in the faded grass,
The beetle's wings are folded mute,
　Where the steps of the idler pass.

4

The widow donned her russet robe,
  Her cap of snowy hue,
And o'er her staid maternal form
  A sober mantle threw;
And she, while fresh the morning light,
  Hath gone to pass the day,
And ease an ailing neighbour's pain
  Across the meadow way.

5

Young Eva closed the cottage door;
  And wooed by bird and flower,
She loitered on beneath the wood,
  Till came the noon-tide hour.
The sloping bank is cool and green,
  Beside the sparkling rill;
The cloud that slumbers in the sky,
  Is painted on the hill.

The spirits poised their purple wings
　　O'er blossom, brook and dell,
And loitered in the quiet nook
　　As if they loved it well.
Young Eva laid one snowy arm
　　Upon a violet bank,
And pillow'd there her downy cheek
　　While she to slumber sank.

7

A smile is on her gentle lip,
　　For she the angels saw,
And felt their wings a covert make
　　As round her head they draw.
A maiden's sleep, how pure it is!
　　The innocent repose
That knows no dark nor troublous dream,
　　Nor love's wild waking knows!

A huntsman's whistle; and anon
   The dogs come fawning round,
And now they raise the pendent ear,
   And crouch along the ground.
The hunter leaped the shrunken brook,
   The dogs hold back with awe,
For they upon the violet bank
   The slumbering maiden saw.

A reckless youth was Albert Linne,
   With licensed oath and jest,
Who little cared for woman's fame,
   Or peaceful maiden's rest.
Like things to him, were broken vows—
   The blush, the sigh, the tear;
What hinders he should steal a kiss,
   From sleeping damsel here?

10

He looks, yet stays his eager foot;
  For, on that spotless brow,
And that closed lid, a something rests
  He never saw till now;
He gazes, yet he shrinks with awe
  From that fair, wondrous face,
Those limbs so quietly disposed,
  With more than maiden grace.

11

He seats himself upon the bank
  And turns his face away,
And Albert Linne, the hair-brained youth,
  Wished in his heart to pray.
But thronging came his former life,
  What once he called delight,
The goblet, oath, and stolen joy,
  How palled they on his sight!

11

He looked within his very soul,
  Its hidden chamber saw,
Inscribed with records dark and deep
  Of many a broken law.
No more he thinks of maiden fair,
  No more of ravished kiss,
Forgets he that pure sleeper nigh
  Hath brought his thoughts to this?

Now Eva opens her child-like eyes
  And lifts her tranquil head,
And Albert, like a guilty thing
  Had from her presence fled.
But Eva held her kindly hand
  And bade him stay awhile;—
He dared not look upon her eyes,
  He only marked her smile;

14

And that so pure and winning beamed,
  So calm and holy too,
That o'er his troubled thoughts at once
  A quiet charm it threw.
Light thought, light words were all forgot,
  He breathed a holier air,
He felt the power of womanhood—
  Its purity was there.

15

And soft beneath their silken fringe
  Beamed Eva's dovelike eyes,
That seemed to claim a sisterhood,
  With something in the skies.
Her gentle voice a part become
  Of air, and brook, and bird,
And Albert listened, as if he
  Such music only heard.

O Eva! thou the pure in heart,
  Why falls thy trembling voice?
A blush is on thy maiden cheek,
  And yet thine eyes rejoice.
Another glory wakes for thee
  Where'er thine eyes may rest;
And deeper, holier thoughts arise
  Within thy peaceful breast.

Thine eyelids droop in tenderness,
  New smiles thy lips combine,
For thou dost feel another soul
  Is blending into thine.
Thou upward raisest thy meek eyes,
  And it is sweet to thee;
To feel the weakness of thy sex,
  Is more than majesty.

18

To feel thy shrinking nature claim
   The stronger arm and brow;
Thy weapons, smiles, and tears, and prayers,
   And blushes such as now.
A woman, gentle Eva thou,
   Thy lot were incomplete,
Did not all sympathies of soul
   Within thy being meet.

19

Those deep, dark eyes, that open brow,
   That proud and manly air,
How have they mingled with thy dreams
   And with thine earnest prayer!
And how hast thou, all timidly,
   Cast down thy maiden eye,
When visions have revealed to thee
   That figure standing nigh!

Two spirits launched companionless
　　A kindred essence sought,
And one in all its wanderings
　　Of such as Eva thought.
The good, the beautiful, the true,
　　Should nestle in his heart,
Should lure him by her gentle voice,
　　To choose the better part.

And he that kindred being sought,
　　Had searched with restless care
For that true, earnest, woman-soul
　　Among the bright and fair—
He might not rest, he felt for him,
　　One such had been created,
Whose maiden soul in quietude
　　For his call meekly waited.

And oft when beaming eyes were nigh,
   And beauty's lip was smiling,
And bird-like tones were breathing round
   The fevered sense beguiling;
He felt this was not what he sought—
   The soul such mockery spurned,
And evermore with aching zeal,
   For that one being yearned.

And she whose loving soul went forth
   Wherever beauty dwelt;
Who with the truthful and the good
   A genial essence felt,
Oh! often in her solitude,
   By her own soul oppressed,
She fain had nestled like a dove
   Within one stranger breast.

Though higher, holier far than those
  Who listening to her voice,
A something caught of better things,
  That make the heart rejoice;
Yet *teaching* thus her spirit lone
  Aweary would have knelt,
And *learned* with child-like reverence,
  Where deeper wisdom dwelt.

And now that will of stronger growth,
  That spirit firmer made,
Instinctive holds her own in check,
  Her timid footsteps stayed;
And Eva in her maidenhood,
  Half trembles with new fear,
And on her lip that strange, deep smile,
  The handmaid of a tear.

While doubting thus, a seraph stayed
  His radiant course awhile;
And with a heavenly sympathy,
  Looked on with beaming smile:
And thus his words of spirit-love
  Trust and assurance brought,
And bade her where the soul finds birth,
  To weakly question not.

Content to feel—care not to know,
  The sacred source whence its arise—
Respect in *modesty* of *soul*,
  This mystery of mysteries:
Mere mind with all its subtle arts,
  Hath only learned when thus it gazed
The inmost veil of human hearts,
  E'en to themselves must not be raised.

Her trusting hand, then Eva laid
  In that of Albert Linne,
And for one trembling moment turned
  Her gentle thoughts within.
Deep tenderness was in the glance
  That rested on his face,
As if her woman-heart had found
  Its own abiding place.

And when she turned her to depart
  Her voice more liquid grew,
" Dear youth, thy thoughts and mine are one;
  One source their being drew !
And they must mingle evermore ;—
  Thy thoughts of love and me,
Will, as a light, thy footsteps guide
  To life and mystery."

30

And then she bent her timid eyes,
   And as beside she knelt,
The pressure of her sinless lips
   Upon his brow he felt.
Low, heart-breathed words she uttered then :
   For him she breathed a prayer ;
He turned to look upon her face,—
   The maiden was not there. !

PART VII.

Eva hath fulfilled her destiny. Material things can no further minister to the growth of her spirit. That waking of the soul to its own deep mysteries—its oneness with another, has been accomplished. A human soul is perfected. She had moved amid the beings around her one, but unlike them, in the world—but not of it. Those who had felt the wisdom of her sweet teachings, yet felt repelled, as by a sacred influence. They dared not crave companionship with a spirit so lofty, and yet so meek.— And thus, though the crowd, as it were, might press upon her, she was yet alone in her true spiritual atmosphere. To them she became a light, a guide, but to Albert Linne alone, was her mission of Womanhood. In her he learned that no one seeketh in vain, the good and the true—that as our faith is, it is given unto us. He confidently sought for the Divine, and it was given unto him. He but touched her garment and she perceived the soul test.

Sorrow and pain—hope, with its kin-spirit, fear, are not for the sinless. She hath walked in an atmosphere of light, and her faith hath looked within the veil.—

The true woman, with woman's love and gentleness, and trust and childlike simplicity, yet with all her noble aspirations and spiritual discernments, she hath known them all without sin, and sorrow may not visit such. She ceased to be present—she passed away like the petal that hath dropped from the rose—like the last sweet note of the singing-bird, or the dying close of the wind harp. Eva is the lost pleiad in the sky of womanhood. Has her spirit ceased to be upon the earth? Does it not still brood over our woman hearts?—and doth not her voice blend ever with the sweet voices of Nature! Eva, mine own, my beautiful, I may not say—farewell.

/

Twas night—bright beamed the silver moon,
   And all the stars were out;
The widow heard within the dell
   Sweet voices all about.
The loitering winds were made to sound
   Her sinless daughter's name,
While to the roof a rare toned-bird
   With wondrous music came.

And long it sat upon the roof
   And poured its mellow song,
That rose upon the stilly air,
   And swelled the vales along.
It was no earthly thing she deemed,
   That, in the clear moonlight,
Sat on the lowly cottage roof,
   And charmed the ear of night. (*d*)

The sun is up, the flowerets raise
   Their folded leaves from rest;
The bird is singing in the branch
   Hard by its dewy nest.
The spider's thread, from twig to twig,
   Is glittering in the light,
With dew-drops has the web been hung
   Through all the starry night.

4

Why tarries Eva long in bed,
　　For she is wont to be
The first to greet the early bird,
　　The waking bud to see?
Why stoops her mother o'er the couch
　　With half suppressed breath,
And lifts the deep-fringed eyelid up?—
　　That frozen orb is death!

5

Why raises she the small pale hand,
　　And holds it to the light?
There is no clear transparent hue
　　To meet her dizzy sight.
She holds the mirror to her lips
　　To catch the moistened air:
The widowed mother stands alone
　　With her dead daughter there!

And yet so placid is the face,
   So sweet its lingering smile,
That one might deem the sleep to be
   The maiden's playful wile.
No pain the quiet limbs had racked,
   No sorrow dimm'd the brow,
So tranquil had the life gone forth,
   She seemed but slumbering now.

7

They laid her down beside the brook
   Upon the sloping hill,
And that strange bird with its rare note,
   Is singing o'er her still.
The sunbeam warmer loves to rest
   Upon the heaving mound,
And those unearthly blossoms spring,
   Uncultured from the ground.

8

There Albert Linne, an altered man,
  Oft bowed in lowly prayer,
And pondered o'er those mystic words
  Which Eva uttered there.
That pure compassion, angel-like,
  Which touched her soul when he,
A guilty and heart-stricken man,
  Would from her presence flee;

9

Her sinless lips from earthly love,
  So tranquil and so free;
And that low, fervent prayer for him,
  She breathed on bended knee.
As Eva's words and spirit sank
  More deeply in his heart,
Young Albert Linne went forth to act
  The better human part.

Nor yet alone did Albert strive;
For, blending with his own,
In every voice of prayer or praise
Was heard young Eva's tone.
He felt her lips upon his brow,
Her angel form beside;
And nestling nearest to his heart,
Was she—THE SPIRIT BRIDE.

The Sinless Child, with mission high,
Awhile to Earth was given,
To shew us that our world should be
The vestibule of Heaven.
Did we but in the holy light
Of truth and goodness rise,
We might communion hold with God
And spirits from the skies.

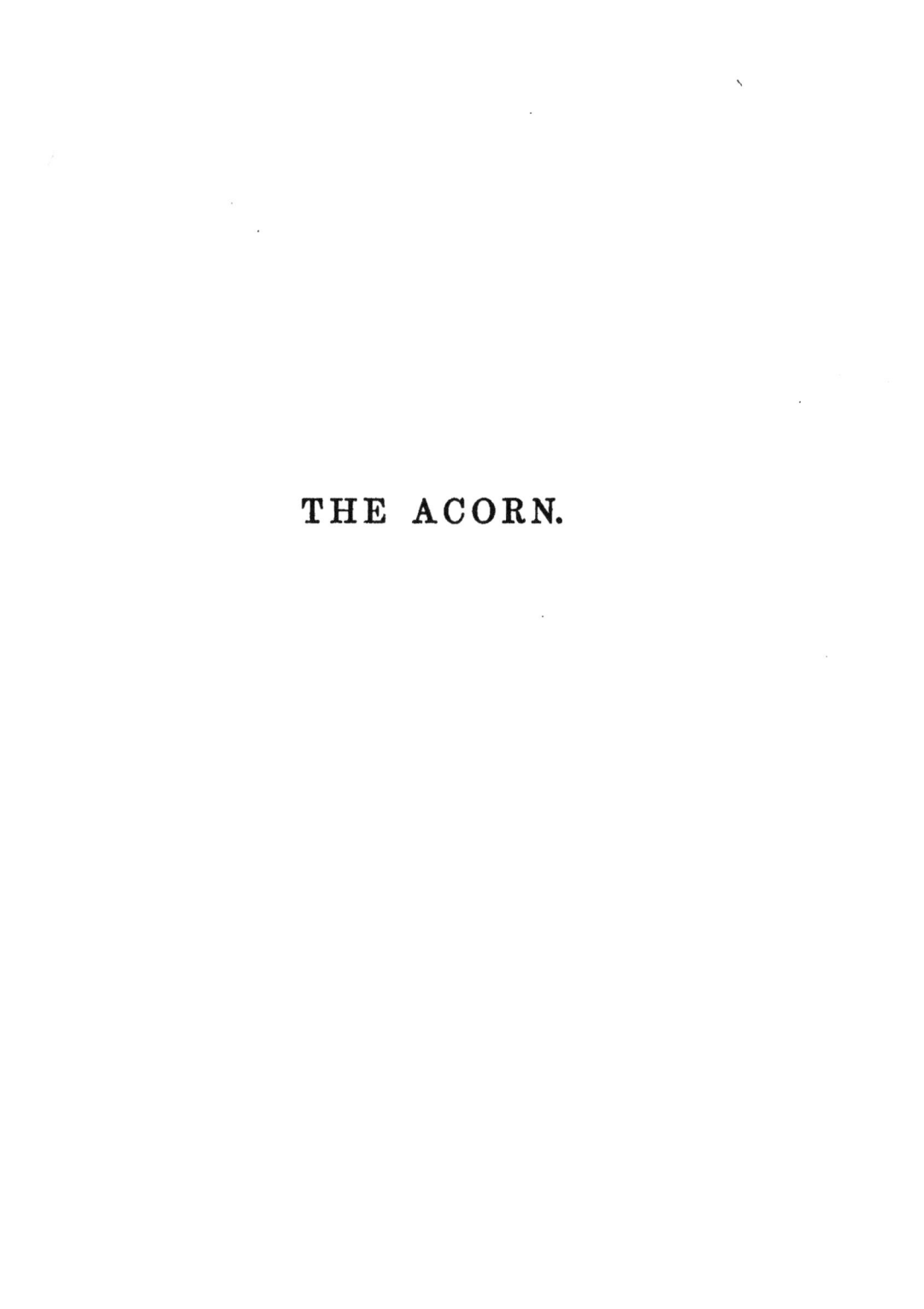

THE ACORN.

THE ACORN.

An acorn fell from an old oak tree,
    And lay on the frosty ground—
" O, what shall the fate of the acorn be !"
    Was whispered all around,
By low-toned voices, chiming sweet,
    Like a floweret's bell when swung—
And grasshopper steeds were gathering fleet,
    And the beetl's hoofs up-rung—

For the woodland Fays came sweeping past
    In the pale autumnal ray,
Where the forest leaves were falling fast,
    And the acorn quivering lay;
They came to tell what its fate should be,
    Though life was unrevealed;
For life is holy mystery,
    Where'er it is conceal'd.

They came with gifts that should life bestow:
    The dew and the living air—
The bane that should work its deadly wo—
    Was found with the Fairies there.
In the gray moss-cup was the mildew brought,
    And the worm in the rose-leaf roll'd,
And many things with destruction fraught,
    That its fate were quickly told.

But it needed not; for a blessed fate
    Was the acorn's doomed to be—
The spirits of earth should its birth-time wait,
    And watch o'er its destiny.
To a little sprite was the task assigned
    To bury the acorn deep,
Away from the frost and searching wind,
    When they through the forest sweep.

I laughed outright at the small thing's toil,
    As he bow'd beneath the spade,
And he balanced his gossamer wings the while
    To look in the pit he made.
A thimble's depth it was scarcely deep,
    When the spade aside he threw,
And roll'd the acorn away to sleep
    In the hush of dropping dew.

The spring-time came with its fresh, warm air,
    And its gush of woodland song;
The dew came down, and the rain was there,
    And the sunshine rested long;
Then softly the black earth turn'd aside,
    The old leaf arching o'er,
And up, where the last year's leaf was dried,
    Came the acorn-shell once more.

With coil'd stem, and a pale green hue,
    It look'd but a feeble thing;
Then deeply its roots abroad it threw,
    Its strength from the earth to bring.
The woodland sprites are gathering round,
    Rejoiced that the task is done—
That another life from the noisome ground
    Is up to the pleasant sun.

THE ACORN.

The young child pass'd with a careless tread,
 And the germ had well-nigh crush'd,
But a spider, launch'd on her airy thread,
 The cheek of the stripling brush'd.
He little knew, as he started back,
 How the acorn's fate was hung
On the very point in the spider's track
 Where the web on his cheek was flung.

The autumn came, and it stood alone,
 And bow'd as the the wind pass'd by—
The wind that utter'd its dirge-like moan
 In the old oak sere and dry;
And the hollow branches creak'd and sway'd
 But they bent not to the blast,
For the stout oak tree, where centuries play'd
 Was sturdy to the last.

A schoolboy beheld the lithe young shoot,
  And his knife was instant out,
To sever the stalk from the spreading root,
  And scatter the buds about;
To peel the bark in curious rings,
  And many a notch and ray,
To beat the air till it whizzing sings,
  Then idly cast away.

His hand was stay'd; he knew not why:
  'Twas a presence breathed around—
A pleading from the deep-blue sky,
  And up from the teeming ground.
It told of the care that had lavish'd been
  In sunshine and in dew—
Of the many things that had wrought a screen
  When peril around it grew.

THE ACORN.

It told of the oak that once had bow'd,
    As feeble a thing to see;
But now, when the storm was raging loud,
    It wrestled mightily.
There's a deeper thought on the schoolboy's brow,
    A new love at his heart,
And he ponders much, as with footsteps slow
    He turns him to depart.

Up grew the twig, with a vigour bold,
    In the shade of the parent tree,
And the old oak knew that his doom was told,
    When the sapling sprang so free.
Then the fierce winds came, and they raging tore
    The hollow limbs away;
And the damp moss crept from the earthy floor
    Around the trunk, time-worn and gray.

The young oak grew, and proudly grew,
    ' For its roots were deep and strong;
And a shadow broad on the earth it threw,
    And the sunlight linger'd long
On its glossy leaf, where the flickering light
    Was flung to the evening sky;
And the wild bird came to its airy height,
    And taught her young to fly.

In acorn-time came the truant boy,
    With a wild and eager look,
And he mark'd the tree with a wondering joy,
    As the wind the great limbs shook.
He look'd where the moss on the north side grew,
    The gnarled arms outspread,
The solemn shadow the huge tree threw,
    As it tower'd above his head:

And vague-like fears the boy surround,
    In the shadow of that tree;
So growing up from the darksome ground,
    Like a giant mystery.
His heart beats quick to the squirrel's tread
    On the withered leaf and dry,
And he lifts not up his awe-struck head
    As the eddying wind sweeps by.

And regally the stout oak stood,
    In its vigour and its pride;
A monarch own'd in the solemn wood,
    With a sceptre spreading wide—
No more in the wintry blast to bow,
    Or rock in the summer breeze;
But draped in green, or star-like snow,
    Reign king of the forest trees.

And a thousand years it firmly grew,
    And a thousand blasts defied;
And, mighty in strength, its broad arms threw
    A shadow dense and wide.
It grew where the rocks were bursting out
    From the thin and heaving soil—
Where the ocean's roar, and the sailor's shout,
    Were mingled in wild turmoil—

Where the far-off sound of the restless deep
    Came up with a booming swell;
And the white foam dash'd to the rocky steep,
    But it loved the tumult well.
Then its huge limbs creak'd in the midnight air,
    And joined in the rude uproar:
For it loved the storm and the lightning's glare,
    And the sound of the breaker's roar.

The bleaching bones of the seabird's prey
    Were heap'd on the rocks below;
And the bald-head eagle, fierce and gray,
    Look'd off from its topmost bough.
Where its shadow lay on the quiet wave
    The light boat often swung,
And the stout ship, saved from the ocean-grave,
    Her cable round it flung.

Change came to the mighty things of earth—
    Old empires pass'd away;
Of the generations that had birth,
    O Death! where, where were they?
Yet fresh and green the brave oak stood,
    Nor dreamed it of decay,
Though a thousand times in the autumn wood
    Its leaves on the pale earth lay.

A sound comes down in the forest trees,
    An echoing from the hill;
It floats far off on the summer breeze,
    And the shore resounds it shrill.
Lo! the monarch tree no more shall stand
    Like a watch-tower of the main—
The strokes fall thick from the woodman's hand,
    And its falling shakes the plain.

The stout old oak!—'Twas a worthy tree,
    And the builder marked it out;
And he smiled its angled limbs to see,
    As he measured the trunk about.
Already to him was a gallant bark
    Careering the rolling deep,
And in sunshine, calm, or tempest dark,
    Her way she will proudly keep.

THE ACORN.

The chisel clinks, and the hammer rings,
    And the merry jest goes round;
While he who longest and loudest sings
    Is the stoutest workman found.
With jointed rib, and trunnel'd plank
    The work goes gayly on,
And light-spoke oaths, when the glass they drank,
    Are heard till the task is done.

She sits on the stocks, the skeleton ship,
    With her oaken ribs all bare,
And the child looks up with parted lip,
    As it gathers fuel there—
With brimless hat, the bare-foot boy
    Looks round with strange amaze.
And dreams of a sailor's life of joy
    Are mingling in that gaze.

With graceful waist and carvings brave
　　The trim hull waits the sea—
And she proudly stoops to the crested wave,
　　While round go the cheerings three.
Her prow swells up from the yeasty deep,
　　Where it plunged in foam and spray;
And the glad waves gathering round her sweep
　　And buoy her in their play.

Thou wert nobly rear'd, O heart of oak!
　　In the sound of the ocean roar,
Where the surging wave o'er the rough rock broke
　　And bellow'd along the shore—
And how wilt thou in the storm rejoice,
　　With the wind through spar and shroud,
To hear a sound like the forest voice,
　　When the blast was raging loud!

With snow-white sail, and streamer gay,
    She sits like an ocean-sprite,
Careering on in her trackless way,
    In sunshine or dark midnight:
Her course is laid with fearless skill,
    For brave hearts man the helm;
And the joyous winds her canvass fill—
    Shall the wave the stout ship whelm?

On, on she goes, where icebergs roll,
    Like floating cities by;
Where meteors flash by the northern pole,
    And the merry dancers fly;
Where the glittering light is backward flung
    From icy tower and dome,
And the frozen shrouds are gayly hung
    With gems from the ocean foam.

On the Indian sea was her shadow cast,
    As it lay like molten gold,
And her pendant shroud and towering mast
    Seem'd twice on the waters told.
The idle canvass slowly swung
    As the spicy breeze went by,
And strange, rare music around her rung
    From the palm-tree growing nigh.

O, gallant ship, thou didst bear with thee
    The gay and the breaking heart,
And weeping eyes look'd out to see
    Thy white-spread sails depart.
And when the rattling casement told
    Of many a perill'd ship,
The anxious wife her babes would fold,
    And pray with trembling lip.

The petrel wheeled in her stormy flight;
    The wind piped shrill and high;
On the topmast sat a pale blue light,
    That flickered not to the eye:
The black cloud came like a banner down,
    And down came the shrieking blast;
The quivering ship on her beams is thrown,
    And gone are helm and mast.

Helmless, but on before the gale,
    She ploughs the deep-troughed wave:
A gurgling sound—a phrenzied wail—
    And the ship hath found a grave.
And thus is the fate of the acorn told,
    That fell from the old oak tree,
And the woodland Fays in the frosty mould
    Preserved for its destiny.

SONNETS.

POESY.

With no fond, sickly thirst for fame, I kneel,
Oh, goddess, of the high-born art to thee;
Not unto thee with semblance of a zeal
I come, oh, pure and heaven-eyed Poesy!
Thou art to me a spirit and a love,
Felt ever from the time, when first the earth,
In its green beauty, and the sky above
Informed my soul with joy too deep for mirth.
I was a child of thine before my tongue
Could lisp its infant utterance unto thee,
And now, albeit from my harp are flung
Discordant numbers, and the song may be
That which I would not, yet I know that thou
The offering wilt not spurn, while thus to thee I
    bow.

RELIGION.

Alone, yet not alone, the heart doth brood
With a sad fondness o'er its hidden grief;
Broods with a miser's joy, wherein relief
Comes with a semblance of its own quaint mood.
How many hearts this point of life have passed!
And some a train of light behind have cast,
To show us what hath been, and what may be;
That thus have suffered all the wise and good,
Thus wept and prayed, thus struggled, and were
    free.
So doth the pilot, trackless through the deep,
Unswerving by the stars his reckoning keep,
He treads a highway not untried before,
And thence he courage gains, and joy doth reap,
Unfaltering lays his course, and leaves behind the
    shore.

THE UNATTAINED.

And is this life? and are we born for this?
To follow phantoms that elude the grasp,
Or whatso'er's secured, within our clasp,
To withering lie, as if each mortal kiss
Were doomed death's shuddering touch alone to meet.
O Life! has thou reserved no cup of bliss?
Must still THE UNATTAINED beguile our feet?
The UNATTAINED with yearnings fill the breast,
That rob, for aye, the spirit of its rest?
Yes, this is Life; and everywhere we meet,
Not victor crowns, but wailings of defeat;
Yet faint thou not, thou dost apply a test,
That shall incite thee onward, upward still,
The present cannot sate, nor e'er thy spirit fill.

AN INCIDENT.

A SIMPLE thing, yet chancing as it did,
When life was bright with its illusive dreams,
A pledge and promise seemed beneath it hid;
The ocean lay before me, tinged with beams,
That lingering draped the west, a wavering stir,
And at my feet there fell a worn, grey quill;
An eagle, high above the darkling fir,
With steady flight, seemed there to take his fill
Of that pure ether breathed by him alone.
O! noble bird! why didst thou loose for me
Thy eagle plume? still unessayed, unknown
Must be that pathway fearless winged by thee;
I ask it not, no lofty flight is mine,
I would not soar like thee, in loneliness to pine!

LIFE.

SUGGESTED BY COLE'S FOUR PAINTINGS REPRESENTING THE VOYAGE OF LIFE.

CHILDHOOD.

Thou poet-painter, preacher of great truth,
Far more suggestive thine than written tome—
Lo, we return with thee to that vast dome,—
Dim cavern of the past. Visions uncouth,
Vague, rayless, all impalpable in sooth,
Send back the startled soul. The waters come
All tranquilly from that dim cavern forth,
The mystic tide of human life. A child,
Borne on its bosom, sports with blossoms wild.
A Presence, felt, but still unseen, the boat
With gentle hand guides onward, and beguiled
With music lost in other years, they float
Upon the stream. The hours unfelt, for life
Is joy in its first voyage, with light and blossoms
    rife.

YOUTH.

Alas, the Spirit lingers, but its hand
No more the barque sustains. The daring youth
Has seized the helm, and deeper launches forth,
His eye amid illusions of ideal land—
Bright castles, built in air, fame, glory, worth,
Fabrics, that still receding, seem to stand;
He sports no more mid blossoms of green earth;
He hears no more the music of his birth;
The future lures him, pinnacles and towers,
And half he chides the lagging of the hours,
Unheeds their sunshine, blessedness and mirth;
For onward is his course, he asks not where,
Since fancy paints the prospect passing fair.

MANHOOD.

Still onward goes the barque—the tide
Bears it along where breakers foam and roar,
And oaks unbending, riven, line the shore;
Dense vapors rising, all the future hide;
And how shall he that future peril bide?
The guiding helm he eager grasps no more;
Time weighs the prow, the wave is deep beside;
Swift flows the current, fierce the gathering strife,
The struggle and the buffetings of life.
Half he recoils, yet calmly bides the test,
With hands clasped firmly on the unconquered
    breast;
Nor meets alone that hour with peril rife;
Forth from on high the guardian Spirit bends
With ministry of love, and holy valour sends.

OLD AGE.

Thy mission is accomplished—painter—sage,
Look to thy crown of glory—for thy brow
Is circled with its radiant halo now.
No more earth's turmoil will thy soul engage,
Its hopes unquiet, littleness, or rage.
With thine own voyager thou hast heard the sound
Of that vast ocean, waveless, rayless, dread,
Where time's perpetual tribute, circling round,
Drops silent in, all passionless and dead.
When thine own voyage is o'er, and thou shalt near
The eternal wave, thus, thus above thy head
May opening glories shield thy heart from fear;
A child again, but strong in faith and prayer,
Thou shalt look meekly up—behold thy God is there!

A DREAM.

I DREAMED last night, that I myself did lay
Within the grave, and after stood and wept,
My spirit sorrowed where its ashes slept!
'Twas a strange dream, and yet methinks it may
Prefigure that which is akin to truth.
How sorrow we o'er perished dreams of youth,
High hopes and aspirations doomed to be
Crushed and o'ermastered by earth's destiny!
Fame, that the spirit loathing turns to ruth;—
And that deluding faith so loth to part,
That earth will shrine for us one kindred heart!
Oh, 'tis the ashes of such things that wring
Tears from the eyes—hopes like to these depart,
And we bow down in dread o'ershadowed by
  death's-wing!

THE BARD.

It cannot be, the baffled heart, in vain,
May seek, amid the crowd, its throbs to hide;
Ten thousand others kindred pangs may bide,
Yet not the less will our own griefs complain.
Chained to our rock, the vulture's gory stain,
And tearing beak is every moment rife,
Renewing pangs that end but with our life.
Thence bursteth forth the gushing voice of song,
The soul's deep anguish thence an utterance finds,
Appealing to all hearts: and human minds
Bow down in awe: thence doth the Bard belong,
Unto all times: and this, O this is fame—
He asked it not: his soul demanded bread,
And ye, charmed with the voice, gave but a stone
       instead.

[The writer's first passage up the Hudson was on a tranquil night at the close of summer, a clear moonshine making the stars pale in the deep sky. Nothing could exceed the loveliness of the scene, as doubling point after point, the river at each turn revealed a new aspect of beauty. It was no longer the majestic Hudson, sweeping its proud waters to the ocean, bearing a fleet upon its bosom, and making a grand highway for wealth and luxury; but a graceful, sentient creature, with an onward purpose, gliding amid the hills, and smiling as it overcame the obstacles in its path.]

TO THE HUDSON.

OH! river, gently as a wayward child,
   I saw thee 'mid the moonlight hills at rest,
Capricious thing, with thine own beauty wild,
   How did'st thou still the throbbings of thy breast!

Rude headlands were about thee, stooping round
   As if amid the hills to hold thy stay;
But thou did'st hear the far-off ocean sound,
   Inviting thee from hill and vale away,
To mingle thy deep waters with its own;
   And, at that voice, thy steps did onward glide,
Onward from echoing hill and valley lone;
   Like thine, oh, be my course—nor turned aside,
While listing to the soundings of a land,
   That like the ocean call invites me to its strand.

NOTES.

NOTES

TO THE SINLESS CHILD.

(*a*) "There was neither hammer nor axe, nor any tool of iron, heard in the house while it was building."

1 Kings, chap. vi. verse 7.

(*b*) It is a common belief among the vulgar, that a sigh always forces a drop of blood from the heart, and many curious stories are told to that effect; as for instance, a man wishing to be rid of his wife, in order to marry one more attractive, promised her the gift of six new dresses, and sundry other articles of female finery, provided she would sigh three times every morning before breakfast, for three months. She complied, and before the time had expired, was in her grave. Many others of a like nature might be recorded. The old writers are full of allusions of a like kind, particularly Shakspeare, "blood consuming sighs," &c.

(c) The worship of the Madonna is in the true spirit of poetry. She became to the christian world what the Penates had been to the classical. In confining ourselves to the abstractions of religion, we run the hazard of making it one of thought rather than of emotion. A woman must always worship through her affections, and one may readily conceive the comfort which the household faith in the presence of the Madonna is likely to inspire.

(d) We are indebted to the Aborigines for this beautiful superstition. The Indian believes that if the wekolis or whipporwill alights upon the roof of his cabin and sings its sweet plaintive song, it portends death to one of its inmates. The omen is almost universally regarded in New-England. The author recollects once hearing an elderly lady relate with singular pathos, an incident of the kind. She was blest with a son of rare endowments and great piety. In the absence of his father he was wont to minister at the family altar; and unlike the stern practices of the Pilgrims, from whose stock he was lineally descended, he prostrated himself in prayer in the lowliest humility. It was touching to hear his clear low voice, and see his spiritual face while kneeling at this holy duty.

One quiet moonlight night while thus engaged, the mother's heart sank within her to hear the plaintive notes of the whippoorwill blending with the voice of prayer. It sat upon the roof and continued its song long after the devotions had ceased. The tears rushed to her eyes, and she embraced her son in a transport of grief. She felt it must be ominous. In one week he was borne away, and the daisies grew, and the birds sang over his grave.

CONTENTS.

	PAGE
PREFACE	XV
The Sinless Child	37
The Acorn	141

SONNETS.

Poesy	161
Religion	162
The Unattained	163
An Incident	164
Cole's Paintings of The Voyage of Life,	
Childhood	165
Youth	166
Manhood	167
Old Age	168
A Dream	169
The Bard	170
To The Hudson	171
Notes to The Sinless Child	175

CPSIA information can be obtained
at www.ICGtesting.com
Printed in the USA
LVHW082051040820
662391LV00004B/141